Bindi Irwin

ABDO
Publishing Company

A Big Buddy Book
by **Sarah Tieck**

VISIT US AT
www.abdopublishing.com

Published by ABDO Publishing Company, 8000 West 78th Street, Edina, Minnesota 55439.

Printed in the United States.

Coordinating Series Editor: Rochelle Baltzer
Contributing Editors: Heidi M.D. Elston, Megan M. Gunderson, Marcia Zappa
Graphic Design: Maria Hosley
Cover Photograph: AP Photo: Richard Drew
Interior Photographs/Illustrations: AP Photo: Australia Zoo (page 17), Discovery Network U.S. (page 11), NewsWire via AP Images/Ali Paige Goldstein (page 28), AAP Image/Dave Hunt (pages 14, 17), Steve Holland, (page 15), PA/Myung Jung Kim (page 10), NBC NewsWire via AP Images/Curtis Means (page 26), AAP Image/Tony Phillips (page 7), Seth Wenig (page 21); Getty Images: Australia Zoo via Getty Images (page 27), Steve Granitz (page 5), Mark Grimwade (page 8), Bradley Kanaris (pages 23, 25), Scott Wintrow (page 29); iStockphoto/Anne Clark (page 9); Photos.com (pages 13, 19).

Library of Congress Cataloging-in-Publication Data

Tieck, Sarah, 1976-
  Bindi Irwin / Sarah Tieck.
    p. cm. -- (Big buddy biographies)
  Includes index.
  ISBN 978-1-60453-122-0
  1. Irwin, Bindi, 1998---Juvenile literature. 2. Wildlife conservationists--Australia--Biography--Juvenile literature. I. Title.

QL31.I77T54 2009
590.92--dc22
  [B]
                          2008009357

Contents

Animal Lover

Bindi Irwin is a famous **conservationist**. She and her family are known for their love of animals.

Bindi has appeared in several television shows. She is best known for *Bindi the Jungle Girl*. People around the world have watched it on the Discovery Kids channel.

Sometimes, Bindi appeared on *The Crocodile Hunter* with her parents. Her father was known for saying "Crikey!"

INDIAN OCEAN

PACIFIC OCEAN

AUSTRALIA

NORTHERN TERRITORY

QUEENSLAND

WESTERN AUSTRALIA

SOUTH AUSTRALIA

Beerwah

NEW SOUTH WALES

VICTORIA

TASMANIA

SOUTHERN OCEAN

N W E S

Family Ties

Bindi Sue Irwin was born on July 24, 1998, in Queensland, Australia. Her parents are Steve and Terri Irwin. Bindi has a younger brother named Robert.

The Irwins began teaching Robert and Bindi about conservation at a very young age.

Graham the Crocodile is one of many saltwater crocodiles that live at the Australia Zoo.

Did you know...

In 2004, a series of giant ocean waves hit the island of Sumatra. This tsunami destroyed villages and killed many people. Bindi wanted to help. So, she sent her favorite doll to a girl who lived there.

Aboriginal Australians have a history that dates back to Australia's earliest years.

Bindi is an **Aboriginal** word. It means "little girl." The Australia Zoo had a saltwater crocodile named Bindi. Steve named his daughter after this favored zoo animal.

Bindi often helped her parents with their television show.

Family Adventures

Bindi's family owns the Australia Zoo in Queensland. They make sure the animals there are cared for and happy. When Bindi was born, Steve and Terri were starring in *The Crocodile Hunter*. This popular television show helped people learn about animals.

On *The Crocodile Hunter,* Steve got very close to dangerous animals.

Did you know...

Bindi had her first television shoot when she was just two weeks old! Her parents took her to Texas to do a show on rattlesnakes.

Bindi has traveled to cities such as New York City, New York, and Los Angeles, California. She has also been to natural places such as the Australian Outback. The Australian Outback is a large rural area full of unusual wildlife.

Since she was a baby, Bindi has been traveling the world with her family. Her parents took her along on their adventures. They appeared on many television shows together.

When she is not traveling, Bindi lives in Beerwah, Queensland. At home, she spends a lot of time at the Australia Zoo. Bindi likes to play with her younger brother. She also studies and helps with chores.

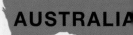
Australian Outback

AUSTRALIA

ARCTIC OCEAN

New York City, New York

UNITED STATES

PACIFIC
OCEAN

ATLANTIC
OCEAN

Los Angeles, California

N
W E
S

Australia Zoo

Fans created a memorial for Steve at the Australia Zoo.

A Sad Day

In 2006, Bindi's life changed. Her father died after an accident. Steve's death saddened people around the world. Thousands of people attended his **memorial** service at the Australia Zoo.

Terri, Bindi, and Robert were very sad, too. But, they decided to continue Steve's work with animals.

Bindi shared stories and memories of her father at his memorial service.

Life at the Zoo

Today, Terri runs the Australia Zoo. Bindi helps her mom care for the animals and do special shows.

Bindi, Terri, and Robert live on zoo property. After work, they are able to walk home.

One of Bindi's favorite animals was Harriet, a giant Galápagos land tortoise.

The Australia Zoo

Bindi's grandparents are Bob and Lyn Irwin. They opened the Australia Zoo in 1970. At first, it was called the Beerwah Reptile Park.

Since 1992, it has been known as the Australia Zoo. There, visitors ride in Steve's Safari Shuttle. Also, they can see shows at the Animal Planet Crocoseum.

Robert attends homeschool with Bindi. But, they study different subjects.

School Days

Bindi attends school at home. This is called homeschooling. She learns from a private teacher.

Homeschooling allows Bindi to travel and shoot television shows. When the family is away from home, Bindi takes a break from her studies. When she's home, she continues her schoolwork.

Did you know...

Bindi has a pet rat named Candy
and a dog named Diamond.

21

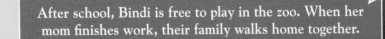

At home, Bindi starts school in the morning. She learns subjects such as math and reading. Bindi also studies piano, **martial arts**, and surfing.

Jungle Girl

Like her dad, Bindi enjoys teaching people about animals. To do this, she travels the world working on television shows. In June 2007, *Bindi the Jungle Girl* **debuted**.

In addition to television, Bindi has been in books, magazines, and newspapers. She also does interviews and gives speeches.

THE JUNGLE GIRL

In 2007, Bindi and Terri appeared in the Macy's Thanksgiving Day Parade. This was a fun way to teach people about animals.

As a **conservationist**, Bindi wants to help save animals. Sometimes people hurt animals or the places they live. Bindi helps people learn about this. Then, they can help save animals too.

Bindi worked with her dad on some episodes of *Bindi the Jungle Girl*.

Buzz

In November 2007, Bindi and Terri were interviewed on the *Today* show.

When she's home, Bindi continues to help at the Australia Zoo. Also, she does schoolwork and spends time with her family.

Like her parents, Bindi wants to spend her life helping animals. She plans to continue doing speeches, **interviews**, and television shows.

28

Did you know...

Bindi has created her own line of clothing! It is called Bindi Wear. Bindi Wear debuted in March 2008.

Bindi is not afraid to pick up snakes or touch lizards!

Snapshot

★ **Name**: Bindi Sue Irwin

★ **Birthday**: July 24, 1998

★ **Birthplace**: Queensland, Australia

★ **Home**: Beerwah, Queensland, Australia

★ **Appearances**: *Bindi the Jungle Girl, Bindi Kidfitness, My Daddy the Crocodile Hunter, The Crocodile Hunter Diaries, The Crocodile Hunter*

Important Words

Aboriginal (a-buh-RIHJ-nuhl) of or relating to the first or earliest-known people to live in Australia.

conservationist a person who works to save land, water, and other natural resources.

debut (DAY-byoo) a first appearance.

interview to ask someone a series of questions.

martial (MAHR-shuhl) **arts** Asian fighting arts, often practiced as sport. Karate and judo are martial arts.

memorial serving as a reminder of a person or an event.

Web Sites

To learn more about Bindi Irwin, visit ABDO Publishing Company on the World Wide Web. Web sites about Bindi Irwin are featured on our Book Links page. These links are routinely monitored and updated to provide the most current information available.

www.abdopublishing.com

Index